Your First
POND

CONTENTS

Front cover painting by:
D A Lish

Photos by:
David Twigg
David Alderton
Dick Mills
Colin Jeal

Illustrations by:
Dick Mills

©1999 by Kingdom Books PO9 5TL ENGLAND

INTRODUCTION

The addition of water to any garden brings an added dimension, providing relaxation, entertainment and quiet enjoyment all through the year. However, people have different ideas about what they want in a pond. One person dreams of a modestly-sized, pre-formed pond with aquatic plants and fountains, while another cannot envisage life without Koi; and such a combination might not always be feasible. Yet another may want a water feature without any fish, or a wildlife pond free of such encumbrances as filters.

The problem with compromises is that they rarely suit every requirement. Only by understanding how the pond works can you hope to get long-term enjoyment from it.

The Nature Pond

Building a nature pond has its own rewards, but converting such a pond later to keep fish isn't always possible.

By definition, nature ponds are designed to attract wildlife. The wildlife using the pond will be seasonal, so the nature pond need not have a filtration system or be built to support aquatic life through winter. Certain design features must be included, such as shallow water, escape ramps for amphibians, and surrounding shrubs or low plants to allow animals to get to and from the pond without fear of predation. The water temperature will not be stable enough to provide fish with a stress-free environment, being too hot in summer and too cold in winter.

The nature pond.

Everyman's Fish Pond

This is how everyone imagines a pond. The water's edge is disguised by flowering marginal plants, water-lilies adorn the surface, and occasionally a fish breaks gently through. A colourful dragonfly flits from plant to plant, while the trickling sound from the cascade or fountain soothes away daily stress.

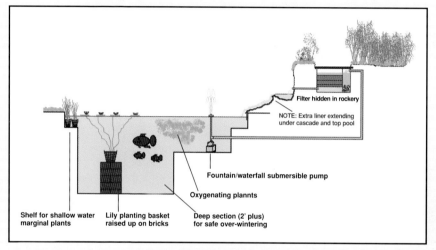

Filter hidden in rockery

NOTE: Extra liner extending under cascade and top pool

Fountain/waterfall submersible pump

Oxygenating plannts

Shelf for shallow water marginal plants

Lily planting basket raised up on bricks

Deep section (2' plus) for safe over-wintering

Everyman's pond.

Creating this vision requires careful planning. The pond must be sited so that the plants receive the correct amount of sunshine. The water depth should be such that the overall volume of water offers stable conditions (the bigger the better); there should be both deep and reasonably shallow parts of the pond; shelves for marginal plants are usually incorporated into the designs of pre-formed ponds but should be planned for when you are implementing your own design.

The Raised Pond

This pond is much the same as the 'in-ground' pond, but it does have distinct advantages. First there is no back-breaking hole to dig – just a few back-breaking loads of bricks and cement to carry! Real advantages include increased safety both for children and for the infirm. A slippery surround can be very treacherous, but drownings in raised ponds are rare. Again, pond maintenance is so much easier: there is no bending down over water and, if seats are incorporated into the pond wall, much of the maintenance can be carried out sitting down.

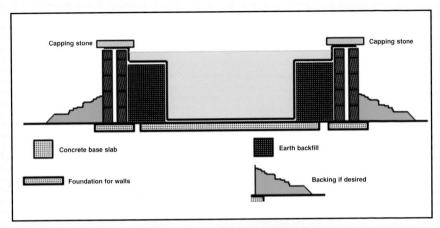

Raised pond using rigid pre-formed pond.

A raised pond.

A compromise design is the semi-raised pond, where one face of the pond is exposed through a vertical face such as a wall, perhaps with a window incorporated into it. This proves an ideal way of installing a pond on sloping land; some ponds can be arranged in tiers and connected by falling cascades over-spilling into each other.

The Koi Pond

A pond for Koi is, if you'll pardon the phrase, a very different kettle of fish. The minimum depth of the pond must be more than 1.5m (5ft), as opposed to the more normal 60–90cm (24–36in) depth of the Goldfish pond. Koi are hearty eaters, so not many plants survive in the pond, and there's a proportional amount of waste product! As a result, the water becomes very polluted and depends heavily on the efficiency of the pond's filtration system to keep conditions within safe limits. During construction, it is normal for bottom drains and side ports to be built into the base and walls of the pond for efficient cleaning and filtering.

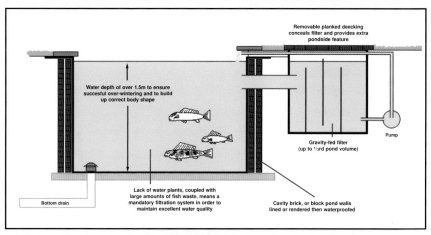

The Koi pond.

In Summary...

You can see that careful planning is needed for any type of pond. Most manufacturers offer catalogues with good advice sections. Draw up a list of your needs and a site plan. Visit a specialist water garden centre, as knowledgeable staff can go through your plans with you and advise on all aspects of your dream pond. The rest is up to you.

DESIGN

Location

You would imagine that the first priority is to put the pond where it will look best — a hardly-used corner of the garden or under some trees. However, a normal fish and plants pond needs plenty of sunlight to reach its full potential, which rather excludes the above situations.

Trees have other drawbacks. If the trees or shrubs are young when the pond is installed, their roots will extend, and could puncture the pond liner or even disturb the foundations of a concrete pond. Every year you will have to net out leaves and berries, which could contaminate the water in the pond. However, a pond needs protection against extreme weather conditions, and windbreaks provided by a nearby hedge or fence could be advantageous. Many marginal plants grow quite tall, and a strong wind can soon topple them into a pond, spoiling the planned effect.

It's very pleasant to sit on the patio or look from indoors through a window at a nearby pond. One distinct advantage of having the pond near the house is that power and water supplies are at hand and no lengthy pipework needs to be installed. However, siting the pond that close to the house might mean that, at certain times of day, vital sunlight is prevented from reaching the pond.

If the site slopes, you could use the gradient in your water garden design. Link two pools by a stream or cascade, or set the pond into the slope and hold it back with a decorative retaining wall or grassy bank. Take care to prevent ground water from running down a sloping lawn into the pond, especially if you have used fertilisers or weedkillers.

Materials

The choice of materials is between concrete, ready-made, pre-formed pond 'shells' or sheet lining material.

Concrete can be used if the ground is stable, with little risk of subsidence, and the design is formal. However, curving designs make concrete more difficult to use and any ground subsidence is likely to crack it. Also, concrete needs to be 'sealed' once set so that any lime in its mixture does not leach out to contaminate the pond water, and this lengthens the process.

Pre-formed ponds, usually made from reinforced glass-fibre, are much quicker to install. All you need is a hole dug to the correct shape and depth. You are limited by what is available commercially, however.

Sheet lining material does not restrict you in any way. You can excavate the hole in the ground (or construct an above-ground box) to whatever size or shape you wish and line it with the material to make it watertight. For larger ponds, you can have widths of liner welded together to your specifications. Use the most expensive material you can afford as this will last the longest – the best materials often have a guarantee for 20 years or more. The cheapest materials, such as thin

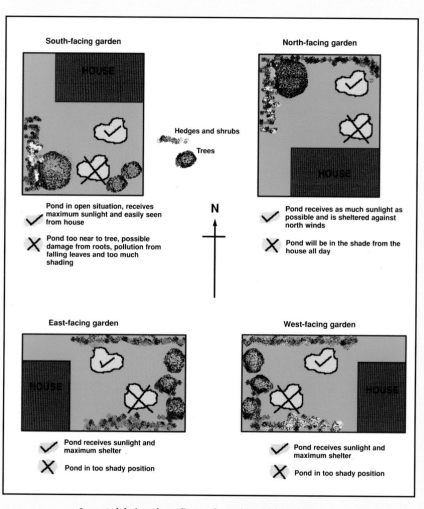

Suggested designs depending on the position of the garden.

plastics, become brittle or degrade because their 'above water' areas are exposed to ultra-violet rays from the sun in summer and the effect of frosts in winter. The thicker sheetings of butyl or synthetic rubber are much more robust.

Necessary Calculations

Before starting you must assess how much material you require. For concrete, refer to more specialist books on pond construction but, as far as lining material is concerned, the rule is straightforward:

> The maximum length of the liner should be equal to the maximum length of the pond plus twice the maximum depth.
> The maximum width of the liner should be equal to the maximum width of the pond plus twice the maximum depth.

This gives a liner that covers the hole and allows an overlapping edge to anchor the liner around the pond. The overlap can be hidden under the lawn or pond-side paving slabs.

The Nature Pond

A simple, shallow hole fitted with liner material is quite adequate for a nature pond. Maximum depth need not be more than 46cm (18in), and gently sloping sides with very shallow beach areas are ideal. Leave room around the pond for sheltering shrubs and half-immerse inclined objects in the water to act as ladders for animals to get into (and out of) the pond. No fountain or filtration system need be installed.

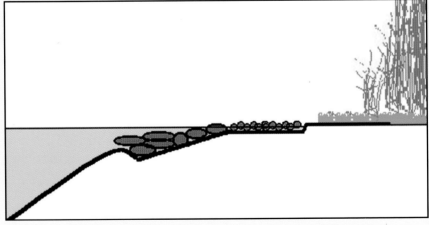

Beach effect achieved by creating a shallow wide shelf and filling with pebbles of graduated sizes.

A half-raised pond.

Fish and Plants Pond

This type of pond can be formal or informal. Avoid too many curves and kinks as they can cause problems when you are trying to hide overlapping wrinkles in the lining material and create stagnant, stationary bodies of water.

The pond should have a maximum depth of 60–76cm (24–30in) somewhere in its design, but leave shelves 15cm (6in) wide and 23cm (9in) deep around the circumference on which to site marginal plants. A filter must be incorporated into the plans, which can be either in the pond or nearby, so allow space for it. If you intend to develop the water garden later to include a pond-side bog garden, plan this when you install the main pond. Also consider how you are going to provide electricity to power fountains, filters, lights and waterfalls.

Koi Pond

The Koi pond is where things get serious! The water depth needs to be at least 1.2–1.5m (4–5ft) over most of the pond. One way around all that extra digging is to make the Koi pond half-in, half-out of the ground. Making it a semi-raised pond has other benefits. Its more hazardous water depth is made safer by virtue of the raised pond sides and, if a pergola is built onto the walls, the overhead screening hides the pond from the view of any passing heron.

Because Koi require excellent quality water conditions and have a habit of eating water plants that would otherwise help to keep things that way, a filtration system is essential. This is best provided as an external filter chamber alongside the pond; it will be described in more detail elsewhere (see FILTRATION).

LABOUR

Whichever form of pond you wish to install, there is no quick and easy way to do it.

Raised Ponds

All that is needed is a brick box, which is then lined in the usual way. The main labour here lies in carrying heavy materials around.

In-Ground Ponds

With an in-ground pond the site has to be prepared, the hole dug (think how you will dispose of the excavated soil), drains laid, and the pond lined or concreted. We will assume that an informally-shaped in-ground liner pond has been the choice of design, but installation of a pre-formed rigid glass-fibre pond follows much the same principles.

First draw out on the ground the shape of the pond, using a length of rope or hose-pipe or a trail of sand. A pre-formed pond's outline can be traced by running a sharpened length of wood, held vertically, around the pond's rim. Don't invert the pond onto the ground and draw around it unless the outline is symmetrical or you'll end up digging the hole the wrong way round. Ready-made ponds always look much bigger when viewed leaning up against a wall in the garden centre than when installed in your garden. Don't just view the pond outline from ground level – go indoors and look out of an upstairs window to get the whole thing in proportion.

The finished pond must be level; otherwise varying expanses of liner will be exposed, detracting from the pond's appearance. Once you start digging away soil, check and recheck constantly that you are keeping things level. A long board with a spirit-level midway can straddle opposite parts of the pond.

If the pond is to have a paved surround, remove a section of turf slightly wider than the planned surround from around the pond's outline. Dig down about 10cm (4in) and lay a firm base of rubble and concrete so that the paving slabs will be level with the surrounding turf. When the outside ring of concrete has set, dig out a layer of soil about 23–30cm (9–12in) deep across the whole pond area inside the perimeter. Re-trace the outline of the pond about 15–23cm (6–9in) inside the original outline. The area inside the two outlines will form a continuous shelf on which marginal plants can be placed.

A beautiful pond with well thought-out contour and shading.

Continue digging out the central area of the pond, remembering to have a maximum depth of 46-60cm (18–24in) somewhere in the design. By removing less soil you can have shallower parts, even a gradually-sloping beach area.

When you have finished digging, you can install drainage pipes, but in the average fish and plants pond this is not mandatory. If you are using a pre-formed pond the base of the excavation must be absolutely level and may require a slab of concrete to provide a firm base.

To protect the liner from puncture damage from stones or tree roots, pre-line the hole with a 5cm (2in) layer of sand, applied slightly damp for easier shaping. Old carpets, newspapers or commercially-available 'pond underlay' material can also be used.

Lay out the liner material across the pond, weighing down its edges with a few stones to keep it roughly in place. As water is fed into the pond through a hose-pipe its weight will pull the liner down into the shape of the excavated hole. You need to get into the pond and, with your bare feet, direct the liner into the desired shape, carefully smoothing out any large wrinkles. Don't forget to move the stones from the edges to allow movement of the liner.

For a pre-formed pond, position it on its concrete slab. Backfill the space between the pond shell and the surrounding excavated hole firmly with earth as you run water into the pond. Keep tamping the earth down and checking that the pond lip is level.

When the pond is full, pull back the edges of the liner over the concrete surround, or stretch it across the earth if turf is to be replaced right up to the pond, and trim. There is no need to treat the concrete surround as the covering layer of liner will prevent any lime from leaching into the pond.

If the pond water has become excessively dirty it should be emptied and refilled. Brush any dirt from the liner as the water level falls. It is a good idea to know just how much water is in the pond, particularly when you are adding treatments for water conditioning or to cure diseases. Use a flowmeter (which you can probably hire from your pond dealer) to measure the water as it flows into the pond; this one-off measurement will stand you in good stead for many years to come.

The paved pond surrounds can be put into position with dabs of mortar beneath each stone. Try to arrange a very slight slope away from the pond across the slabs so that rainwater does not run into the pond. Hide the liner by letting the stones project over the water surface for 5cm (2in) or so. This also helps to protect it from damage from the sun's ultra-violet rays. If you are installing a submersible pond pump, introduce the electricity supply cable between two stones before pointing in the stones with mortar. Site the pump near to any water returning from a waterfall or cascade, to prevent undue water currents occurring in the pond, as these would upset water-lily growth.

Before introducing fish to the pond, treat the water with a dechlorinating agent and let the pond stand for a week or two. You can plant the pond immediately.

As the pond will be raised above ground, the pond sides are being built with bricks.

Water Features
Fountains

A fountain is simple to install; the most difficult part is making sure that the jets are level with, and just above, the water surface.

Fountain kits are available from your aquatic dealer. Those for smaller fountains (in terms of water flow) may only provide a decorative jet above the pond surface. More powerful kits include the option of feeding the water from the submersible pump to another feature (such as a waterfall or filter) as well as providing the fountain jet.

Waterfalls and Cascades

Waterfalls and cascades are often used to disguise or enhance the appearance of water returning to the pond from an external filtration system (see FILTRATION). Waterfalls and cascades can be made by cementing together pieces of stones to your own design, or purchased ready-made in fibre-glass or reconstituted stone. The one vital thing to bear in mind with either form is that watercourses are renowned causes of water loss from the pond. Pond liner material must be placed under all the stones used in the construction to ensure that all spilt water is channelled back to the pond. Water is also lost through the action of the surrounding terrestrial plants, whose overhanging shoots siphon water out of your carefully-created stream. On windy days, the spray from fountains often returns to the surrounding lawn rather than the pond.

Inter-Connecting Water Features

For those with sloping garden sites, ponds interconnected by streams become a real possibility, although such designs can also be made quite successfully in a flat environment. All that is needed is a deep sump from which water is pumped to ground surface level to trickle along a shallow gravel bed to the pond and to the sump again before being re-circulated.

Pumps

It is important that the correct size of pump is used to achieve the required effect. To produce a thin, continuous sheet of water over a 15cm (6in) wide sill of stone, a minimum of 1365 litres (298 gallons) of water per hour is required. However, it is no use just buying a pump of this capacity; you must consider the maximum height to which the water has to be lifted before running back down the waterfall and the amount of pipework, including its diameter and the number of bends in its route. All these factors offer extra resistance to the pump's efficiency and must be allowed for. When burying pipework, feed the pipe through a non-crushable rigid-plastic outer pipe such as is used for cold-water installations.

Pumps can be operated by either full mains voltage electricity or the safer, lower voltage of 24V. In either case, buried armoured cable and water/weather-proofed junction boxes and switches should be used for the supply to the pump.

You must calculate the distance the water has to be raised.

FILTRATION

A pond is not exactly a self-cleaning proposition, although frequent rain and the action of aquatic plants can do much to keep things from becoming too bad. You can help by installing a filtration system, which needn't be as technically difficult as you might think.

Principles of Pond Filtration

The idea couldn't be simpler – to pass water through some device to clean it and then return it to the pond. In most cases this involves physically taking water from the pond but there are now filters that sit in the pond water itself, obviating the need for external devices.

There are three ways of cleaning water – mechanically, chemically and biologically.

Mechanical filtration involves straining out suspended materials from the water. This is achieved by passing the water through brushes, foam blocks or sheeting of various densities. In multi-chambered external filters, this process is usually the first. Unfortunately, simple mechanical filtration will not clear greenness from pond water without the addition of an ultra-violet lamp (see SEASONAL CARE – Summer).

Chemical filtration removes dissolved substances from the water and is achieved by the use of activated carbon to absorb unwanted impurities. Filters using activated carbon are generally used to treat the tap water before it is fed into the pond, although this is used more frequently in aquarium set-ups.

Biological filtration is perhaps the most important of all. It employs bacteria to break down toxic substances such as ammonia into less harmful compounds and generally occurs in the final section of the filter system.

Practicalities

If you have a pond pump running a fountain, you can usually use it to feed water from the pond to an external filter containing the necessary filter medium and let gravity bring the water back to the pond via a waterfall or cascade (see LABOUR – Water Features).

A drawback of this system is that this type of pump is not capable of passing solid materials up to the filter box. Additionally, the pump's impeller often liquidises any suspended dirt into much finer particles that do not get trapped in the filter foam. The pump is also fitted with a strainer to protect the pump against particles of grit, and this tends to become clogged very frequently. One solution is to use a more suitable submersible pump that can handle solids without being damaged.

An alternative is to sink the filter chamber into the ground next to the pond. Water passes to the filter by a pipe through the side wall of the pond, is filtered, and then the clean water is pumped back to the pond. The advantages of this system are that all dirty water reaches the filter and the pump is only asked to pump clean water, without having to pump it to any height.

In-pond filters are filter boxes filled with appropriate media as before but sunk in the pond and connected to the input of the pump. Obviously this unit takes up some pond space but it avoids the need to run extra pipework and hide the filter in the rockery. There is a submersible version of an ultra-violet clarifier, so none of your pond's water treatment system needs to be visible.

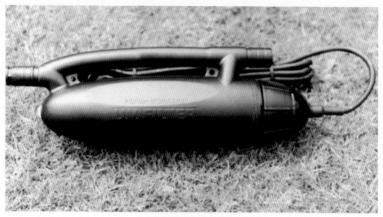

A submersible UV filter.

Care of filters

Mechanical trapping media such as brushes and foam must be rinsed out periodically to maintain optimum water flow. On the other hand, cleaning out the biological filter medium only destroys the very bacteria colony that is doing all the work. The best way is to rinse it in some of the pond water, rather than raw tap water, which would most certainly kill off any beneficial bacteria that have established themselves even in non-biological filter areas.

During winter, many pond-keepers turn off their filtration systems. This means that in the spring the filter must re-establish itself before the bacteria get to work again. To hasten this process, you can buy filter maturation fluids (cultures of the bacteria) that get your filter up and running in the shortest possible time.

PLANTS

An important 'ingredient' in pond water is oxygen and most of this enters through the water surface directly from the atmosphere. However, the supply of oxygen can be supplemented by living, submerged plants, which produce oxygen as a by-product of photosynthesis. More importantly, during this process the plants remove carbon dioxide, thus keeping water conditions sweet. The plants that perform this vital service are known collectively as oxygenators and can be purchased from the aquatic store or garden centre.

Water-lilies, apart from adding colour and shade to the pond, remove nutrients from the water, which otherwise would be quickly taken up by single-celled plants (algae) that produce the bright green water conditions during spring and summer.

All water-lilies are sold as young plants and have a tuberous root (rhizome). They should be planted in pots and placed in the pond so that any existing leaves are floating on the surface. You may have to stand the pot on some bricks to achieve this and gradually reduce the height of the pot support as the plant grows.

Marginal plants are those which like (or tolerate) standing with their roots in water. Plant them in pots around the pond to soften its outline and provide welcome shelter for visiting insects and animals.

A bog garden next to the pond gives colour to the pond surround, although the plants in this section prefer moist rather than permanently-waterlogged soil. A bog area is quite easy to install: it's almost the same as digging out a pond, but the liner used to retain the moisture should be punctured to allow the water to disperse slowly.

Never add soil to the bottom of the pond and plant into it. Many pond plants are very invasive and will take over a pond in no time at all. Use individual planting baskets so that the plants are contained and stay where you want them.

When introducing bunches of oxygenators to the pond, float them in the shallow water until growth is seen. These oxygenators need not be planted in pots; they are quite happy to float free in the water. Fish may nibble at them but, since their growth is rapid, this doesn't matter.

Don't install tall marginal plants, as they may be blown into the pond.

Submerged Plants

Most of the species described live under water, taking their nourishment directly through the leaves; roots are used as anchorages rather than for food collection. Many oxygenators can be propagated easily by taking cuttings.

Curly Pondweed (*Potamogeton crispus*) The leaves of this plant have curled, wavy edges; dark red and white flowers are held just above the water surface during summer. This plant makes very rapid growth, especially if it can get its roots into some mud, so keep it in check.

Elodea (*Lagarosiphon major*) Growth of the stems bearing the tightly-curled leaves is vigorous and the plant may need regular thinning out.

Hornwort (*Ceratophyllum demersum*) The fine leaves of this plant make an excellent spawner medium for goldfish, whose eggs are easily trapped within the mass of leaves. Young fry find shelter, also.

Willowmoss (*Fontinalis antipyretica*) The stems of this plant, with their very tiny dark green leaves, cling to underwater stones rather than rooting in compost. An excellent spawning medium for fish.

Water Chestnut (*Trapa natans*) This plant has dark-coloured leaves arranged in a diamond shape, held just below the surface. Another fast grower, given enough sun.

Water Hawthorn (*Aponogeton distachyos*) The long oval leaves are held on the surface very much like those of the water-lily. The white flowers are scented.

Water Hyacinth (*Eichhornia crassipes*) Many people are attracted to this plant by the bulbous growths at the base of the leaves, which serve as buoyancy chambers. Flowers are pale violet, but require lots of sunshine to develop. This plant is more tropical than temperate and will not survive frosts.

Water Soldier (*Stratiotes aloides*) This 'now you see it, now you don't' plant has spiky leaves radiating from a central point. It rises and falls in the water; some say according to season, others according to water condition.

Developing blanketweed.

Water-Lilies (Nymphaea varieties)

Aim to provide shade for the fish by covering a third of the surface of the pond with water-lily leaves. Make a note of the depth of water each species needs and choose the most suitable for your pond rather than selecting the colour you like best. Many water-lilies grow too large (in surface area coverage terms) for the average garden pond. A typical selection for the medium-sized pond would be:

Ellisiana rich red; **Gonnere** white; **James Brydon** wine-red; **Nymphaea x helvola** yellow, ideal for small ponds; **Rose Arey** pink

Marginal Plants

Water Violet (*Hottonia palustris*) The stiffly-held stems bear small lilac-coloured flowers above the water surface. The plant soon forms clumps. Another species, *Hottouynia cordata*, has white flowers and almost heart-shaped leaves. The plant does well in both wet and moist conditions.

Irises These moisture-loving plants can be grown both in water and in boggy ground. There are many suitable varieties, featuring several colours. A popular species, *Iris ensata* (formerly *I kaempferi*), has clematis-shaped leaves.

Parrot's Feather (*Myriophyllum aquaticum*) The aptly-named feather-like pale green leaves are held stiffly above the water surface and make an excellent feature for the pond perimeter.

Water-lily.

Marsh Marigolds.

Marsh Marigold (*Caltha palustris*) The bright yellow buttercup-like flowers of this plant add contrasting colour to the pond side.

Juncus (*Juncus effusus*) has a wild-looking tangly spiral growth which forms a clump. *Juncus ensifolia* is distinguished by small, dark-brown spherical flowerheads amongst the upright stiff leaves.

Plants For The Bog Garden

Astilbe The feather-duster appearance of the flowers adds both movement and colour. Several colours are available, the pink variety Venus being very popular. The flower heads can be left on the plant during winter.

Gunnera This large, rhubarb-like plant has a spiky stem and grows to an enormous size. Choose it only if you have room. In winter, cover the crown of the plant by folding over the large leaves.

Hosta The shapes, sizes and colours (some variegated) of leaves of these predominantly foliage plants are commonly featured as pond-side decorations where the moisture is entirely to their liking.

Primula The primula group offers flowers of several colours, ranging from red to yellow. The species *Primula vassilli* looks a little like a miniature 'red hot poker', except that the colours of the flowers are purple and red.

FISH

A pond for fish and plants with a maximum depth of 46–60cm (18–24in) is not suitable for Koi; only for Goldfish and some other fish from temperate zones. The recommended stocking level is 1cm of fish body length (don't count the tail) for approximately 400 sq cm of water surface area. (In imperial units, this is very roughly equivalent to one inch of fish body length to one square foot of water.) Build up to this slowly, as stocking less allows for the fish to grow and breed!

Goldfish

Many varieties of Goldfish (*Carassius auratus*) are available from your aquarist but not all are suitable for the outdoor pond. You should restrict your choice to those known as single-tails. Fish with divided tail fins (making them look double or 'twin-tailed') are generally unsuitable because their egg-shaped bodies make manoeuvring in the outside pond more difficult, and their over-developed or accentuated fins may become congested in pond water, especially if conditions are not at their best. The Common Goldfish is an excellent pond fish. Its bright orange-red metallic colouration is easily seen as it glides amongst the plants.

The Comet, another slim metallic-scaled fish, has a much larger tail (often almost as long as its body) and can shoot off at high speed – not very helpful when you try to catch it. A popular colour variant has a red 'cap' to the top of the head, contrasting vividly with a white body.

The Bristol Shubunkin has scales that look opaque and carry many colours – violet, blue, brown, black, red and orange among them, but its claim to fame is its developed tail with its large rounded lobes. The London Shubunkin has the same slim body and colouration but the tail remains short, as in the basic Common Goldfish.

Bristol Shubunkin.

Other Coldwater Fish

Golden Orfe (*Idus idus*) This slim fish with a golden top above silvery sides spends much of its time at the water surface, where it cruises about in a relaxed shoal. It has a habit of leaping during summer, either through high spirits or as it catches insects, which, in small ponds, means it ends up on the lawn.

Tench (*Tinca tinca*) This fish is a dull-coloured greeny-brown in its natural state and spends all its time foraging on the pond floor. Although the Golden and Red-and-white Tench (both cultivated varieties) are available they are not frequently seen. You can be sure of seeing Tench only when you clean the pond out in autumn and find them in the sludge at the bottom!

The Common Goldfish.

Red Shiner (*Cyprinella lutrensis*) From North America, this attractive fish with its red and purple colouration will be quite happy in the pond. Its small size might make it less visible, however, and pond-keepers might find it a more attractive proposition for the indoor coldwater aquarium.

Pumpkinseed (*Lepomis gibbosus*) This fish can reach 25cm (10in), making it more suitable for a pond than for even a large aquarium. Its oval, golden-brown-green body reflects many iridescences, and its face is marked with blue streaks. Unlike many fish, it does not scatter eggs haphazardly but excavates a nest, usually about 30cm (12in) in diameter, into which up to 1000 eggs can be laid.

Golden Orfe.

Tench.

Medaka (*Oryzias latipes*) This small, yellow-golden, oriental fish can be kept in the pond all year round and can often be seen swimming about, even below a layer of ice. Again, this fish has an interesting breeding pattern: fertilised eggs hang like bunches of grapes from the female's body until they are brushed off by the aquatic plants, into which they fall and later hatch.

SEASONAL CARE

Autumn

As the leaves fall during autumn, the fish become less active and need less food, although they need to build up their fat resources to see them through winter. At this time, they may prefer a more easily-digestible food based on wheatgerm to the high-protein diet of the summer months. Too much food only pollutes the water. Generally, do not feed pond fish once temperatures are consistently below 10°C (50°F).

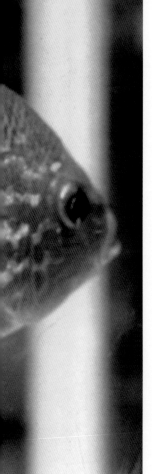

Leaves falling from trees and the dying back of aquatic plants may pollute the pond. Decaying vegetation uses up vital oxygen and produces unwanted gases such as methane and hydrogen sulphide. It is a good idea to clean out all decaying matter from the pond before winter.

Winter

Take care once ice covers the pond. If the pond has not been cleaned, the decaying processes continue and the gases cannot escape, so the fish may suffer. It is important to keep the pond ventilated during winter to allow any gases to escape and let oxygen in. An area of the surface should be kept ice-free by floating a ball on the surface, installing a small floating pond heater, or covering the pond with bubble-wrap. Do not break the ice with a hammer, as this would certainly cause the fish some distress. The pump can be switched off, removed from the pond, cleaned and stored, but remember that things will take time to return to their full efficiency in the spring (see FILTRATION – Care of filters).

Spring

Rising temperatures cause pond life to start up. As in autumn, the fish may prefer the easily-digested food before switching over to the main summer diet. Do not rush into full feeding until temperatures rise above 10°C (50°F), even if the fish seem active.

Fish are now at their most vulnerable, as it takes time for their natural immune systems to regain their full capabilities. Do not rush out and buy more fish at this stage; the filtration system may not be able to cope with the added waste load and your fish are probably under a little stress and liable to pick up any disease that may be lurking.

Left: Pumpkinseed.

Summer

Various problems beset the pond-keeper each summer. The worst two are green water and blanketweed, which appear in late spring and all through summer – just when you want to see the pond looking its best.

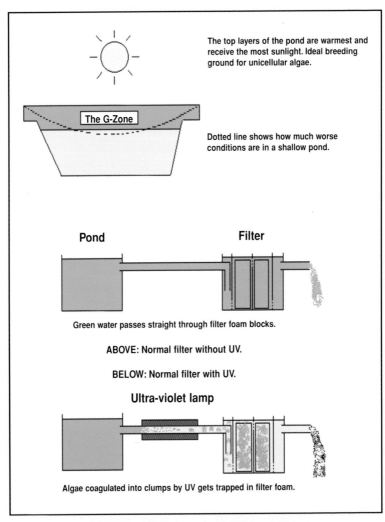

The top layers of the pond are warmest and receive the most sunlight. Ideal breeding ground for unicellular algae.

The G-Zone

Dotted line shows how much worse conditions are in a shallow pond.

Pond   Filter

Green water passes straight through filter foam blocks.

ABOVE: Normal filter without UV.

BELOW: Normal filter with UV.

Ultra-violet lamp

Algae coagulated into clumps by UV gets trapped in filter foam.

How green water develops.

Developing duckweed.

Green water This condition is caused by millions of algae encouraged to grow by sunshine and nutrients. The sunshine gets to work on the water in spring, and nutrients (often encouraged by the fact that you have not cleaned out the pond in the previous autumn) feed the primitive algae in the absence of established aquatic plants. Green water is not unhealthy to fish, but it's unsightly to us.

Passing the green water through a filter system won't remove it. The current method is to incorporate an ultra-violet clarifier into the filtration system. The ultra-violet rays cause the algae to clump together in lumps sufficiently large to be trapped in the filter medium. Renew the ultra-violet lamp each season as it has a limited effective life.

Blanketweed Just as you get the pond water free of green water the blanketweed appears. There are several ways of dealing with this, although no one way appears to be universally effective.

Stocking the pond with vegetarian fish isn't always successful. Many people see Goldfish and Koi apparently eating the blanketweed, and assume the fish will clear it in due course. In reality, all the fish are doing is feeding on small, waterborne creatures living amongst the green filaments.

A powerful magnet, or some electrically-powered polarising coil, in the pipework of the filtration system has been advocated, but this does not always appear to succeed. Water composition (which differs from area to area) evidently has an important bearing on results.

A real favourite is to immerse a small sachet of barley straw in the pond, preferably near the water returning from the filter, to cause the blanketweed to die off. The treatment time may be some weeks, a second sachet being substituted after a month. It is also advisable to lift out the sachet periodically to expose it to the air. Again, it may work better in some areas than others.

The only widely-accepted remedies for blanketweed appear to be vigilance and hard manual work – removing it by hand as soon as it appears. Blanketweed makes an excellent mulch/fertiliser for the garden, so don't waste it!

Duckweed (*Lemna minor*) This small, bright green floating plant is introduced accidentally, carried by a visiting creature or brought in on another water plant. It spreads very rapidly and should be removed as soon as it is seen. Direct the growth to the side by trailing a rope across the surface or spraying it with a high-pressure hose, and then collect it in a net.

Oxygen levels During summer, oxygen levels in the water may drop because of the increase in water temperature. As oxygenators go into reverse at night, absorbing oxygen and giving off carbon dioxide, the pond may become depleted of oxygen during the warmer nights. This is especially likely to happen where there is an abundance of oxygenating plants, so clear some out. Poor oxygen conditions can also be alleviated by keeping the fountain running or trickling water from a hose through the pond while hot, humid conditions persist.

A pond covered with Willowmoss.

BIBLIOGRAPHY

KOI AND GARDEN POOLS
A Complete Introduction
Dr Herbert R Axelrod
ISBN 0-86622-398-3
CO-040
This introduction to the Koi pond includes unique coverage of the microscopic life which is so important to the well-being of the pond and the fish in it. Every popular colour variety of Koi is illustrated.
Hardcover: 208 x 124mm, 128 pages, over 100 full-colour photographs and illustrations.

John Dawes's
BOOK OF WATER GARDENS
ISBN 0-86622-662-1
H–1104
One of the most helpful things for anyone tackling a project is to understand why a particular task should be done in a certain way. John Dawes explains in simple terms the reasons behind the advice he gives as he goes through every aspect of making and keeping a pond, from initial planning to the finished feature.
Hardcover: 220 x 285mm, 176 pages, 211 full colour illustrations plus many drawings and charts.

THE PERFECT POND
RECIPE BOOK
Peter J May
ISBN 185279007-5
GB 002
An easy-to-follow pictorial hand-book to help any would-be pond owner avoid the pitfalls and problems associated with pond construction and design. This is an excellent hands-on and 'how-to-do-it' book.
Hardcover: 250 x 170mm, 32 pages, full colour illustrations throughout.

THE PROFESSIONAL'S
BOOK OF KOI
Anmarie Barrie
ISBN 0-86622-528-5
TS-158
A wonderful introduction to the world of Koi, this book discusses everything that Koi need in order to thrive and be healthy.
Hardcover: 250 x 170mm, 160 pages, 150 full colour photographs and drawings.